SCHOOL CUSTODIANS

Cindy Klingel and Robert B. Noyed

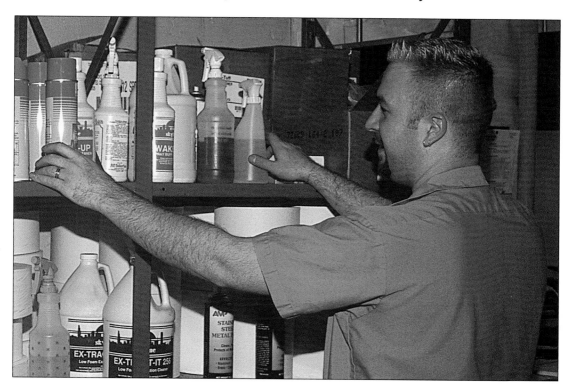

The Rourke Press, Inc.
Vero Beach, Florida 32964

PHOTO CREDITS
© Flanagan Publishing Services/Romie Flanagan

We would like to thank the students and staff of Channing Memorial
School for their valuable assistance in producing this book.

Library of Congress Cataloging-in-Publication Data

Klingel, Cynthia Fitterer
  School custodians / Cindy Klingel, Robert B. Noyed.
    p. cm. — (My school helpers)
  Includes index.
  Summary: Describes a school custodian's job, as he gets the school ready for
the day, checking the heat, clearing icy sidewalks, and making sure that
everything is safe and clean.
  ISBN 1-57103-326-2
  1. School custodians—Juvenile literature. [1. School custodians.
2. Occupations.] I. Noyed, Robert B. II. Title.

LB3235 .K55 2001
371.6'8—dc21
                                     99-059285
                                         CIP

Printed in the USA

CONTENTS

About the Authors

Cindy Klingel has worked as a high school English teacher and an elementary teacher. She is currently the curriculum director for a Minnesota school district. Writing children's books is another way that continues her passion for sharing the written word with children. Cindy Klingel is a frequent visitor to the children's section of bookstores and enjoys spending time with her many friends, family, and two daughters.

Bob Noyed started his career as a newspaper reporter. Since then, he has worked in communications and public relations for more than fourteen years for a Minnesota school district. He enjoys writing books for children and finds that it brings a different feeling of challenge and accomplishment from other writing projects. He is an avid reader who also enjoys music, theater, travelling, and spending time with his wife, son, and daughter.

The person you know best at school is probably your teacher. But many other school helpers keep the school running. You may not know about all they do. Here are some of the many things your school custodian does.

It is very early in the morning. Everything is dark. The first person to arrive at the school is the custodian. He also unlocks the school doors. The custodian's job is to take care of the school and keep it clean.

When the school custodian arrives, it is early morning and still dark.

5

The custodian arrives at school before the teachers and students. He checks the hallways and classrooms and turns on the lights. It is the custodian's job to get the school ready for the school day.

The custodian makes sure that everything is ready for the students and teachers.

The custodian checks the temperature of the building. It is his job to make sure it is not too hot or too cold. The custodian needs to know how to operate the heating and cooling **equipment** in the school. He also may need to fix the equipment when it breaks.

The school custodian is responsible for the school's equipment.

The custodian has to take care of many things in the school building. He replaces burned out lights in the classrooms. He also makes sure that the **fire alarms** are working properly.

Schools have many lights that need to be replaced.

The custodian keeps each classroom clean. Children in the classroom can help by keeping the rooms tidy! It is his job to empty the trash cans from each classroom. The custodian also sweeps or vacuums the floor.

Students sometimes help custodians keep things orderly.

After students and teachers arrive, the custodian has many jobs in other parts of the building. He needs to set up the cafeteria before lunch. Schoolchildren help the custodian by cleaning up after they have eaten. The custodian then has to move all the tables and clean up the room after lunch has been served.

When students clean up after themselves the custodian's job is a little easier.

After lunch, the custodian checks to make sure he has everything he needs to keep the school clean. He makes a list of cleaning **supplies** that need to be ordered.

The school custodian keeps track of the cleaning supplies.

The custodian checks in with the principal of the school. He finds out about special things that are happening in the school. Sometimes the custodian has to set up chairs and other equipment for concerts and sports events.

A custodian puts away mats in the gym to prepare for a special event.

Trucks bring many boxes to the school. It is the custodian's job to help unload and **deliver** the boxes to the right place in the school.

Many students do not realize how much work the custodian does. When students and teachers leave for the day, custodians still have many hours of work to do. Keeping a school clean and safe is an important job.

A custodian unloads boxes.

FURTHER INFORMATION

Books

Flanagan, Alice K., and Christine Osinski. *Call Mr. Vasquez. He'll Fix It!* Danbury, Conn.: Children's Press. 1996

Kaiman, Bobbie D. *School from A to Z.* New York:Crabtree Publishing Co., 1999

Roop, Peter, and Connie Roop. *A School Album.* Chicago Heinemann, 1998

Web Sites
American School Directory

http //www.asd.com/
Locate your own school's web site.

A custodian's job is to clean the school and make it safe.

GLOSSARY

deliver (dee LIV er) — to bring

equipment (ee KWIP ment) — tools

fire alarms (FEYER all ARMS) — bells or sounds that warn people of a fire

supplies (sah PLYZ) — things that are given out when needed

INDEX